Spring Harvest Bible Workbook

THE MISSION OF GOD

Jenny Baker

Series editor for thematic workbooks – Jeff Lucas

Equipping the Church for action

First Published in 2003 Spring Harvest Publishing Division and Authentic
Reprinted 2003, 2008

14 13 12 11 10 09 08   9 8 7 6 5 4 3

Authentic Media
9 Holdom Avenue, Bletchley, Milton Keynes, Bucks, MK1 1QR
1820 Jet Stream Drive, Colorado Springs, CO 80921, USA
OM Authentic Media, Medchal Road, Jeedimetla Village,
Secunderabad 500 055, A.P., India
www.authenticmedia.co.uk
Authentic Media is a division of IBS-STL U.K., limited by guarantee, with
it's Registered Officeat Kingstown Broadway, Carlise, Cumbria CA 0HA.
Registered in England & Wales No. 1216232. Registered charity 270162

The right of Jenny Barker to be identified as the Author of this Work has been asserted by
her in accordance with Copyright, Designs and Patents Act 1988

British Library Cataloguing in Publication Data

A catalogue record for this book is available from the British Library

ISBN 978-1-85078-500-2

Typeset by Spring Harvest
Cover design by Diane Bainbridge
Printed in Great Britain by Bell and Bain Ltd., Glasgow

CONTENTS

ABOUT THIS BOOK

This study book looks at the story of the Exodus and what the liberation of the Israelites from the oppression of Egypt tells us about the Mission of God. Rather than a verse-by-verse exposition, this guide picks out key themes from the story that reveal the nature of the God that we worship. Each session has a passage from Exodus as a focus, but you will need to be familiar with the first twenty chapters of the book of Exodus in order to get the most from the studies. Fortunately, they don't take long to read and it's a gripping story!

This book is written primarily for a group situation, but can easily be used by individuals who want to study the issues it covers. It can be used in a variety of contexts, so it is perhaps helpful to spell out the assumptions that we have made about the groups that will use it. Groups can have a variety of names – homegroups, Bible study groups, cell groups – we've used housegroup as the generic term.

▶ The emphasis of the studies will be on the application of the Bible. Group members will not just learn facts, but will be encouraged to think 'How does this apply to me? What change does it require of me? What incidents or situations in my life is this relevant to?'

▶ Housegroups can encourage honesty and make space for questions and doubts. The aim of the studies is not to find the 'right answer', but to help members understand the Bible by working through their questions. The Christian faith often throws up paradoxes. Events in people's lives may make particular verses difficult to understand or believe. The housegroup should be a safe place to express these difficulties.

▶ Housegroups can give opportunities for deep friendships to develop. Group members can be encouraged to talk about their experiences, feelings, questions, hopes and fears. They can offer one another pastoral support and get involved in each other's lives.

▶ There is a difference between being a collection of individuals who happen to meet together every Wednesday and an effective group who bounce ideas off each other, spark inspiration and creativity, pool their talents and resources to create solutions together and whose whole is definitely greater than the sum of its parts. The process of working through these studies will encourage healthy group dynamics.

Space is given for you to write answers, comments, questions and thoughts. This book will not tell you what to think, but will help you to discover the truth of God's word through thinking, discussing, praying and listening.

FOR GROUP MEMBERS

▶ You will probably get more out of the study if you spend some time during the week reading the passage and thinking about the questions. Make a note of anything you don't understand.

▶ Pray that God will help you to understand the passage and show you how to apply it. Pray for other members in your group too, that they will find the study helpful.

● Be willing to take part in the discussions. The leader of the group is not there as the expert with all the answers. They will want everyone to get involved and share their thoughts and opinions.

● However, don't dominate the group! If you are aware that you are saying a lot, make space for other people to contribute. Be sensitive to other group members and aim to be encouraging. If you disagree with someone, say so without putting down their contribution.

FOR INDIVIDUALS

● Although this book is written with a group in mind, it can also easily be used by individuals. You obviously won't be able to do the group activities suggested, but you can consider how you would answer the questions and write your thoughts in the space provided.

● You may find it helpful to talk to a prayer partner about what you have learned, and ask them to pray for you as you try to apply what you are reading to your life.

The New International Version of the text is printed in the book. If you usually use a different version, then read from your own Bible as well.

Other titles in this Spring Harvest Bible Studies series:

Sermon on the Mount – ISBN 1-85078-407-8
Based on the Spring Harvest 2000 theme, King of the Hill.

Jesus at the Centre – ISBN 1-85078-440-X
Based on the Spring Harvest 2001 theme, A Royal Banquet.

Letters to the Churches – ISBN 1-85078-441-8
Based on the Spring Harvest 2002 theme, You've Got Mail.

Big Themes from Colossians – ISBN 1-85078-457-4
Based on the Spring Harvest 1999 theme, Across the Borderline.

David – After God's Own Heart – ISBN 1-85078-497-3
Based on selected chapters from Ian Coffey's book,
The Story of David, ISBN 1-85078-485-X.

Jonah – God's Compassion – ISBN 1-85078-508-2
Studies on Jonah.

Moses – Friend of God – ISBN 1-85078-519-8
Studies on Moses.

Connect! Workbook – ISBN 1-85078-521-X
Based on Tim Jeffery and Steve Chalke's ground-breaking book rethinking mission for the 21st century.

INTRODUCTION TO THE MISSION OF GOD

The story of the Exodus has all the ingredients of a blockbuster film – confrontation, a battle between good and evil, a showdown between the hero and his nemesis and a decisive victory, with the potential for the special effects department to go to town.

But Exodus is not just a good story, nor is it just the biography of the Prince of Egypt, amazing though Moses' story is. This is the story of the King of Heaven and his mission to call out a people faithful to his name and whose lives reflect his character.

The book of Exodus contributes foundational ideas for an understanding of the mission of God. It is not the only biblical source on God's mission, nor does it tell the whole story: but it is a rich, dramatic account of God's dealings with humanity, and as such has plenty to teach us. We approach the text as Christians, not as Jews, so we will look at the text in the light of Christ, asking what the death and resurrection of Jesus add to our understanding of what it means to be the people of God.

Our journey through Exodus will not be a systematic verse-by-verse, chapter-by-chapter exegesis. We will look at the realities of the mission of God as Moses discovered them. The heart of it all is God's passion and mercy, which is expressed in salvation and freedom: in response to this there is a call to a lifestyle of justice and hope and the whole is entrusted to the church as a 'cycle' in which worship and community both extend and fulfill God's mission. These eight key themes run through the text like threads in a rich, multi-coloured tapestry. They do not claim to be a comprehensive 'menu' of the mission of God. God's mission is wide. There really isn't anything outside its scope, so no list of eight words will ever do it justice. The eight themes we have chosen, though, do begin to give a flavour of the breadth and majesty of God's mission. We have selected them because they are important aspects of the mission of God, and because:

- They are all present and evident in the call of Moses and the subsequent events of the Exodus.
- They are all clearly present and evident in the life, death and resurrection of Jesus.
- They are all relevant to the lives we lead in the contemporary world: not just for the leaders of churches and the strategists of mission, but for all of us as we work, rest and play in the light of God.

PASSION

AIM: To introduce the overall theme of these Bible studies – the Mission of God
To discover more of God's passion for his people and of our place in mission

During that long period, the king of Egypt died. The Israelites groaned in their slavery and cried out, and their cry for help because of their slavery went up to God. God heard their groaning and he remembered his covenant with Abraham, with Isaac and with Jacob. So God looked on the Israelites and was concerned about them.

Now Moses was tending the flock of Jethro his father-in-law, the priest of Midian, and he led the flock to the far side of the desert and came to Horeb, the mountain of God. There the angel of the LORD appeared to him in flames of fire from within a bush. Moses saw that though the bush was on fire it did not burn up. So Moses thought, "I will go over and see this strange sight—why the bush does not burn up."

When the LORD saw that he had gone over to look, God called to him from within the bush, "Moses! Moses!"

And Moses said, "Here I am."

"Do not come any closer," God said. "Take off your sandals, for the place where you are standing is holy ground." Then he said, "I am the God of your father, the God of Abraham, the God of Isaac and the God of Jacob." At this, Moses hid his face, because he was afraid to look at God.

The LORD said, "I have indeed seen the misery of my people in Egypt. I have heard them crying out because of their slave drivers, and I am concerned about their suffering. So I have come down to rescue them from the hand of the Egyptians and to bring them up out of that land into a good and spacious land, a land flowing with milk and honey—the home of the Canaanites, Hittites, Amorites, Perizzites, Hivites and Jebusites. And now the cry of the Israelites has reached me, and I have seen the way the Egyptians are oppressing them. So now, go. I am sending you to Pharaoh to bring my people the Israelites out of Egypt."

But Moses said to God, "Who am I, that I should go to Pharaoh and bring the Israelites out of Egypt?"

And God said, "I will be with you. And this will be the sign to you that it is I who have sent you: When you have brought the people out of Egypt, you will worship God on this mountain."

Exodus 2:23–3:12

God is passionate about the future he has for his people, and will act for their liberation and salvation. Exodus is a story of passion...

TO SET THE SCENE

In what contexts do we use the word mission today? Think of characters in films, songs or examples from everyday life that talk about 'mission'. Produce a group definition of the word mission.

Read the passage together.

1 Tell the story of Moses up to this meeting with God at the burning bush – how did he get here? What relationship does he already have with God?

WHAT DOES SEARCH THE BIBLE SAY? **2** Moses may not have known much about God, but he is about to find out what God is like. Exodus 2:23-25 uses four verbs for the way that God responds to the Israelites – what are they?

God_____ God_____
God_____ God_____

What does this tell us about God's character?

3 In 1998, Dreamworks produced the animated film The Prince of Egypt, which tells the story of the Exodus. But is this story just about Moses?

According to the Bible, who is the real hero of this story?

WHAT DOES SEARCH THE BIBLE SAY? **4** Theologians use the term *Missio Dei* – the Mission of God – to capture this sense of God being a missionary. Can you think of other stories in the Bible where God takes the initiative to seek out men and women?

HOW DOES THIS APPLY TO ME **5** What difference does it make to your perspective to see mission as first and foremost the Mission of God? What role does this give the church in mission?

6 The story of the Exodus fits into the bigger picture of the Bible. God tells Moses at the burning bush, 'I will be with you.' What is the ultimate expression of 'God with us'?

7 Although mission is God's initiative, he involves his people in it. How had Moses' life so far prepared him for his role in God's plan? Did he feel equipped for the task?

HOW DOES THIS APPLY TO ME **8** What can you learn from Moses' story about finding the call of God on your life? Do you have a sense of vocation for your life, of how you can be involved in the Mission of God? What is your advice to others who are looking for a sense of calling? Discuss this first in twos, and then as a group.

Once having the vision, the second step to holy obedience is this: Begin where you are. Obey now. Use what little obedience you are capable of, even if it be like a grain of mustard seed. Begin where you are.

Thomas R. Kelly

WORSHIP

Moses met God at a burning bush; although the bush was on fire, it did not burn up. Light a small fire – in the grate if you have a fireplace inside, outside in the garden if it is dry, or in a barbecue. Give everyone a small piece of wood or a stick and read Exodus 3: 4-10. Ask people to think about how ready they are to be involved in the Mission of God. What excuses might they give to God? How equipped do they feel? Allow people some space to think and pray and then invite them to throw their piece of wood on the fire as a way of saying that they want to be ready to answer God's call to be involved in his mission.

DURING THE WEEK

Sit down with a drink and read the first twenty chapters of Exodus to remind yourself of how God sets his people free from oppression in Egypt. You could also watch a video of The Prince of Egypt. It helps to make some of the characters more real by showing the context in which they were living, but read the Bible version too to understand fully God's role in this great story.

FOR FURTHER STUDY

The four-fold description of God's passion given in Exodus 2:23-25 provides a valuable framework for thinking about mission and prayer.

God hears
The cry of the human heart

God remembers   **God sees**
His people and his promise   The very root of the human condition

God knows
Every detail of our lives

Try applying this framework to an area of concern in your life and mission. How might it change your approach to both mission and prayer if you knew beyond a doubt that, whatever area you are praying or working into, God has heard, remembered, seen and known?[1]

---

[1] This exercise originally appeared in the Spring Harvest *Study Guide 2003, From Shepherd's Bush to King's Cross* by Gerard Kelly.

MERCY

AIM: To understand more of what God is like by examining his actions, and in particular his mercy

But Moses said to God, "Who am I, that I should go to Pharaoh and bring the Israelites out of Egypt?"

And God said, "I will be with you. And this will be the sign to you that it is I who have sent you: When you have brought the people out of Egypt, you will worship God on this mountain."

Moses said to God, "Suppose I go to the Israelites and say to them, 'The God of your fathers has sent me to you,' and they ask me, 'What is his name?' Then what shall I tell them?"

God said to Moses, "I AM WHO I AM. This is what you are to say to the Israelites: 'I AM has sent me to you.'"

God also said to Moses, "Say to the Israelites, 'The LORD, the God of your fathers—the God of Abraham, the God of Isaac and the God of Jacob—has sent me to you.' This is my name forever, the name by which I am to be remembered from generation to generation.

"Go, assemble the elders of Israel and say to them, 'The LORD, the God of your fathers—the God of Abraham, Isaac and Jacob—appeared to me and said: I have watched over you and have seen what has been done to you in Egypt. And I have promised to bring you up out of your misery in Egypt into the land of the Canaanites, Hittites, Amorites, Perizzites, Hivites and Jebusites—a land flowing with milk and honey.'

"The elders of Israel will listen to you. Then you and the elders are to go to the king of Egypt and say to him, 'The LORD, the God of the Hebrews, has met with us. Let us take a three-day journey into the desert to offer sacrifices to the LORD our God.' But I know that the king of Egypt will not let you go unless a mighty hand compels him. So I will stretch out my hand and strike the Egyptians with all the wonders that I will perform among them. After that, he will let you go.

"And I will make the Egyptians favourably disposed toward this people, so that when you leave you will not go empty-handed. Every woman is to ask her neighbour and any woman living in her house for articles of silver and gold and for clothing, which you will put on your sons and daughters. And so you will plunder the Egyptians."

Exodus 3:11–22

God chooses to show mercy to his people, carrying them on eagles' wings to freedom. Exodus is a story of mercy...

TO SET THE SCENE

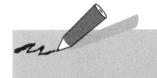

Choose a new name for yourself that says something about you. Borrow a first name from one well-known person with whom you share a skill or an attribute (or aspire to!), and a last name from someone else. You might be David Oliver, a fantastic footballer who is also a great cook, or Anita Radcliffe, a shrewd businesswoman who excels at long-distance running. See if others can guess why you have chosen those names. What names would you choose for each other?

Read the passage together.

1 To the Hebrews, a name was more than just a label, what you called someone. A name contained within itself the character of the person it belonged to, indicating who they really were. What do you think God's name 'I AM WHO I AM' says about his character?

WHAT DOES
SEARCH
THE BIBLE SAY?

2 The name 'I AM WHO I AM' also carries the sense of 'I will be who I will be' – God's nature will be revealed by what he does. Compare God's promises to the Israelites in Exodus 3:7-10 to the way Pharaoh treats them in Exodus 5:5-18. What does this tell us about God's character compared to Pharaoh's?

3   In the light of the New Testament and our place in history, what else does God's action in sending Jesus and Jesus' life, death and resurrection reveal about God's character? Has God stayed consistent to his name and nature as revealed in Exodus?

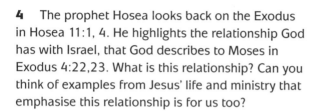

4   The prophet Hosea looks back on the Exodus in Hosea 11:1, 4. He highlights the relationship God has with Israel, that God describes to Moses in Exodus 4:22,23. What is this relationship? Can you think of examples from Jesus' life and ministry that emphasise this relationship is for us too?

5   Some people might say that God is being élitist in choosing only Israel to be his people. What do these passages say about how far his mercy extends (Gen. 12:1-3; Ex. 9:16; Ex. 12:37,38; Mt. 28:18-20; Acts 10:34-36)? How would you answer that accusation of elitism?

HOW DOES THIS / APPLY TO ME

6 God's mercy is expressed in his forgiveness of us. What difference has God's mercy and forgiveness made to your life?

HOW DOES THIS / APPLY TO ME

7 Are there people you struggle to forgive to whom God might long to show mercy? Discuss this in twos, and then share with the whole group – if you are comfortable doing so.

ENGAGING WITH / THE WORLD

8 What new and different activities might you engage in if your definition of mission was 'God using me to show his mercy'?

Returning hate for hate multiplies hate, adding deeper darkness to a night already devoid of stars. Darkness cannot drive out darkness; only light can do that. Hate cannot drive out hate; only love can do that ... Forgiveness does not mean ignoring what has been done or putting a false label on an evil act. It means, rather, that the evil act no longer remains a barrier to the relationship.

Martin Luther King Jr

HOW DOES THIS APPLY TO ME

8 The type of freedom that God won for the Israelites – social, political and spiritual – demonstrates the type of complete freedom he longs to bring to all people who are oppressed and in bondage. Do you think the church still carries that holistic view of freedom, or do we tend to emphasise one aspect over another? How can we make sure that our involvement in the Mission of God brings a holistic freedom to people?

Jesus Christ, God's Son, became a slave, that we who were spiritually enslaved might become sons. Are we living like slaves or like sons?

Mark Stibbe

WORSHIP

Read Exodus 4:24–26. This is a strange event that takes place when Moses is returning to Egypt to confront Pharaoh for the first time. It shows that Moses needed to be right with God before he was able to be involved in the Mission of God. Moses had failed to circumcise his son, which should have been a sign of his commitment to God. Before he could be involved in bringing freedom to the Israelites, he needed to be free himself. There is a personal dimension to spiritual warfare that we ignore at our peril.

Give everyone a piece of string, and ask them to think about areas in their lives where they know they are not completely free – perhaps a relationship that is not right, or a habitual sin or area of weakness. Invite them to tie a knot in the string for each thing that they think of. Then invite people to get into pairs and swap knotted strings. They can talk about what the knots represent if they want to. Ask each person to pray for their partner, unknotting the string as they go, asking God to bring liberation to each area of their life.

DURING THE WEEK

Make a note during the week of every time you are offered something free – it could be a 'buy one get one free offer' at a supermarket, or a free trial of a magazine as long as you sign a direct debit form. What is the motivation behind these offers? How do they compare with the freedom God gives? If they don't match up, spend time thanking God for the nature of the freedom he gives!

FOR FURTHER STUDY

Think about what it must be like to read this story as an Egyptian. It's important to remember that God's battle is not against the Egyptians as an ethnic group, but against the tyrannical regime and evil of Pharaoh. The Egyptians are just as much victims of his evil nature as the Israelites. Tony Campolo illustrates this well in his book, *Let me Tell you a Story*

> *The God we worship is a God who loves all people of all races and tribes... A Hasidic story ... tells of a great celebration in heaven after the Israelites are delivered from the Egyptians at the Red Sea, and the Egyptian armies are drowned. The angels are cheering and dancing. Everyone in heaven is full of joy. Then one of the angels asks the archangel Michael, 'Where is God? Why isn't God here celebrating?' And Michael answers, 'God is not here because he is off by himself weeping. You see, many thousands of his children were drowned today!'*

How does this story affect your attitude to the Egyptians?

SALVATION

AIM: To understand how the salvation of the Israelites from Egypt is a foretaste of the salvation we experience in Christ

As Pharaoh approached, the Israelites looked up, and there were the Egyptians, marching after them. They were terrified and cried out to the LORD. They said to Moses, "Was it because there were no graves in Egypt that you brought us to the desert to die? What have you done to us by bringing us out of Egypt? Didn't we say to you in Egypt, 'Leave us alone; let us serve the Egyptians'? It would have been better for us to serve the Egyptians than to die in the desert!"

Moses answered the people, "Do not be afraid. Stand firm and you will see the deliverance the LORD will bring you today. The Egyptians you see today you will never see again. The LORD will fight for you; you need only to be still."

Then the LORD said to Moses, "Why are you crying out to me? Tell the Israelites to move on. Raise your staff and stretch out your hand over the sea to divide the water so that the Israelites can go through the sea on dry ground. I will harden the hearts of the Egyptians so that they will go in after them. And I will gain glory through Pharaoh and all his army, through his chariots and his horsemen. The Egyptians will know that I am the LORD when I gain glory through Pharaoh, his chariots and his horsemen."

Exodus 14:10–18

God takes action for the rescue of his people: it is by his initiative alone that they are saved. Exodus is a story of salvation...

TO SET THE SCENE
How did you become a Christian? Can you remember a distinct date, or did it happen over a period of time? Was it recently or a long time ago? Was it a dramatic event or a gradual realisation of God's love? Share in twos your stories of how you found salvation, and then with the whole group – but keep it to two minutes each.

Read the passage together.

1   Picture the scene. The Israelites are on their night-time flight from Egypt when they suddenly realise that the Egyptians are coming after them. They are trapped between the desert and the sea, caught like frightened rabbits in the glare of a car's headlights. Read what Moses says to them in Exodus 14:13,14. What central truth about salvation do these words reveal?

WHAT DOES SEARCH THE BIBLE SAY?   **2**   What have the Israelites been saved from (Ex 2:23-25; 5:2)? What have they been saved into – what has changed as a result of their escape from Egypt (Ex 3:17; 4:22,23)?

3   God promised salvation to the Israelites from the first time he spoke to Moses, but it was a while before they received it. What parallels can you see between the Israelites' struggle to be free from Egypt and the way someone might experience God's salvation today?

4   Christian are people of the cross. Whatever we see in the Exodus story of the God who saves, we see more fully in the cross of Christ. Read 2 Corinthians 5:17-21. What does Paul say has been accomplished through the cross?

HOW DOES THIS APPLY TO ME   **5**   Israel received salvation and was also given the task of carrying salvation to other nations. The first Christians were instrumental in bringing thousands to Christ. Paul counted himself as an ambassador for Christ. It seems that we cannot accept God's offer of salvation and then reject his call to mission. How do you feel about that? How effective an ambassador are you?

ENGAGING WITH THE WORLD   **6**   God's salvation is available to all: there is no other way that people can be saved. This is an essential truth of the Christian faith – perhaps the most 'offensive'

HOPE

AIM: To grasp the certainty of the hope God offers to the Israelites and to us

When Pharaoh let the people go, God did not lead them on the road through the Philistine country, though that was shorter. For God said, "If they face war, they might change their minds and return to Egypt." So God led the people around by the desert road towards the Red Sea. The Israelites went up out of Egypt armed for battle.

Moses took the bones of Joseph with him because Joseph had made the sons of Israel swear an oath. He had said, "God will surely come to your aid, and then you must carry my bones up with you from this place."

After leaving Succoth they camped at Etham on the edge of the desert. By day the LORD went ahead of them in a pillar of cloud to guide them on their way and by night in a pillar of fire to give them light, so that they could travel by day or night. Neither the pillar of cloud by day nor the pillar of fire by night left its place in front of the people.

Exodus 13:17–22

By his presence and his promise, God calls his people to a new and different future. Exodus is a story of hope...

TO SET THE SCENE

Discuss what you think the future will be like. Compare the visions of the future that we are often given in films and stories with the expectations that most ordinary people have.

Read the passage together.

1   Once out of Egypt, Israel has to learn that the promises of God are not delivered in an instant. There is a 'now-but-not-yet' dimension to God's plans. What have they already received from all that God has promised, and what still lies in the future (Look back at Ex. 3:7-10 or Ex. 6:6-8)?

2 Their journey to the Promised Land is only just beginning. They need to keep their eyes on the promises of God. What two signs of hope are given in the passage you have just read?

3 Think of the times recently when you have said 'I hope that…' Lesslie Newbiggin writes 'In most ordinary speech hope means little more than a desire of a better future.' Do you agree? What is the difference between a biblical use of the word hope and its use in a sentence like 'I hope it doesn't rain today' (See 1 Pet. 1:3-5; Rom. 5:1-5)?

4 We too can have hope in God's promises because we have Jesus, 'the guarantee of a better covenant' (Heb. 7:22). What other guarantee has God given us (2 Cor. 1:22; 2 Cor. 5:5; Eph. 1:14)?

5 How real is God's presence in your life from day-to-day? What is your 'pillar of cloud' and 'pillar of fire'? Discuss first in twos, and then as a group.

6 How does God's action in your past affect your hope for the future? What has God already done in your life, and what comes into the 'not-yet' category – what are you still hoping for?

7 The Hebrews had to journey through a desert, a physical wilderness where they faced many hardships and had to be dependent on God. Many Christians go through a similar spiritual experience – a time of spiritual exile where God seems distant and life is hard. What do you do to find hope in desert places? What does the patience, provision, protection and presence of God for the Hebrew slaves in their wilderness tell us about what we should look for in ours?

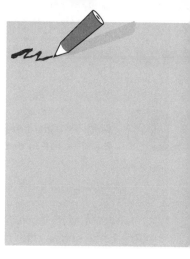

8 Two caricatures of mission are 'turn or burn!' – presenting a horrific view of the future that will scare people into accepting Christ – and 'Come to Jesus and be happy!' – offering a saccharine present that belies the reality of the broken world that we live in. How can we communicate in mission the 'now-and-not-yet' nature of God's promises with the certainty of future hope?

Somehow, in the midst of our tears, a gift is hidden. Somehow, in the midst of our mourning, the first steps of the dance take place. Somehow, the cries that well up from our losses belong to our song of gratitude.

Henri Nouwen

WORSHIP

Think of someone that you know who is going through a desert experience – it might be yourself. Write a prayer, asking God to make his presence known to your friend and hide it in the sand. Take some sand and put it in your pockets – every time you feel it in the coming weeks, it will remind you to pray for that person. Drink some cool water and thank God for his refreshing spirit.

DURING THE WEEK

Think about how you could bless someone this week by reminding them of God's presence and helping to make a future hope more tangible in the present. You could write some words of encouragement to someone that you know is going through a desert experience; you could go and pray with someone in need – after all, prayer is the language of hope.

FOR FURTHER STUDY

Our sense of hope and expectation for the future will depend on our understanding of what God has in store for us. What vision of heaven in given in Revelation 21:1–5? What do you think heaven will be like?

WORSHIP

AIM: To discover the central place of worship in the story of the Exodus and in our lives

Then Moses and the Israelites sang this song to the LORD:

"I will sing to the LORD, for he is highly exalted.
The horse and its rider he has hurled into the sea.
The LORD is my strength and my song; he has become my salvation.
He is my God, and I will praise him, my father's God, and I will exalt him.

The LORD is a warrior; the LORD is his name.
Pharaoh's chariots and his army he has hurled into the sea.
The best of Pharaoh's officers are drowned in the Red Sea.
The deep waters have covered them; they sank to the depths like a stone.

"Your right hand, O LORD, was majestic in power.
Your right hand, O LORD, shattered the enemy.
In the greatness of your majesty you threw down those who opposed you.
You unleashed your burning anger; it consumed them like stubble.
By the blast of your nostrils the waters piled up.
The surging waters stood firm like a wall;
the deep waters congealed in the heart of the sea.

"The enemy boasted, 'I will pursue, I will overtake them.
I will divide the spoils; I will gorge myself on them.
I will draw my sword and my hand will destroy them.'
But you blew with your breath, and the sea covered them.
They sank like lead in the mighty waters.

"Who among the gods is like you, O LORD?
Who is like you—majestic in holiness, awesome in glory, working wonders?
You stretched out your right hand and the earth swallowed them.

"In your unfailing love you will lead the people you have redeemed. In your strength you will guide them to your holy dwelling.

The nations will hear and tremble; anguish will grip the people of Philistia. The chiefs of Edom will be terrified, the leaders of Moab will be seized with trembling, the people of Canaan will melt away; terror and dread will fall upon them. By the power of your arm they will be as still as a stone—until your people pass by, O LORD, until the people you bought pass by.

You will bring them in and plant them on the mountain of your inheritance— the place, O LORD, you made for your dwelling, the sanctuary, O Lord, your hands established.
The LORD will reign for ever and ever."

Exodus 15:1–18

God does not set his people free to wander but to worship. He calls them to himself – to know him, to love him and to honour his name in all the earth. Exodus is a story of worship...

TO SET THE SCENE

Think of a well-known person. Perform the actions that they are well-known for and see if group members can guess who you are pretending to be!

Read the passage together.

WHAT DOES SEARCH THE BIBLE SAY?
1 Having seen the Egyptian army decisively dealt with, the Israelites sing a song of praise and worship to God. Pick out words from these verses that show what have they learned about God's character through their adventure so far.

WHAT DOES SEARCH THE BIBLE SAY?
2 Although there have been some pretty dramatic happenings in this story, we mustn't get distracted by plagues, miracles and destroyed armies. Look at these verses to see how central worship is to the Exodus story: Exodus 3:12; 4:23; 5:3; 15:1-18; 20:1,2; 29: 44-46.

3 Jesus talked about worship in his conversation with the Samaritan woman at the well, and hinted that his coming would herald a change in worship. What was it (Jn. 4:19-26)?

4   Very often worship and mission are seen as separate categories, distinct and unconnected. But in Exodus worship is intertwined with mission and mission is interlaced with worship. Look at the quotes below – what are the links between worship and mission?

I've been challenged on this a lot recently. I say I'm a worship leader, and I also say that worship is far more than just about music. So why are all my acts of worship leading done through music? When it comes to reaching the broken of this world, why am I so often near the back of the queue? I'm longing to be a worshipper who sets an example for others to follow, not just with my lips, but with my life. God has made it very clear that worship and justice are inseparable.

Matt Redman

Unless he is at the centre of all that we do, with actions flowing out of our relationship with him, we might as well shut up our churches and go and join the secular caring agency down the road.

Fran Beckett

Mission is not the ultimate goal of the church. Worship is. Missions exist because worship doesn't. Worship is ultimate, not missions, because God is ultimate, not man. When this age is over, and the countless millions of the redeemed fall on their faces before the throne of God, missions will be no more. It is a temporary necessity. But worship abides forever. Worship, therefore, is the fuel and goal in missions. It's the goal of mission because in mission we simply aim to bring the nations into the white-hot enjoyment of God's glory. The goal of mission is the gladness of the peoples in the greatness of God ... Mission begins and ends in worship.

John Piper

MATERIALS NEEDED

You will need a video of *The Shawshank Redemption*, a TV and video player, or some newspapers; some ice and some clay; and a piece of string for each person.

FEEDBACK

Did anyone pray for God's mercy to be shown in situations during the week?

TO SET THE SCENE

The clip you need to show starts at 1:49:10, ends at 1:54:55 and is 5 minutes and 45 seconds long. (Set the video timer to zero when Tim Robbins' name appears in the credits at the start of the film.) The clip starts just after the prison governor looks into the hole in the wall down which Andy has escaped. Red tells the story – 'In 1966, Andy Dufresne escaped from Shawshank Prison'. It ends after Andy has waded through the river, taken off his shirt and lifted his hands to the sky, rejoicing at his freedom. It has some mild language in it, so you may want to watch it first to check that it will be suitable for your housegroup. When discussing who needs freedom, encourage people to think about different situations where social, political and spiritual liberation are needed. If you do not want to show the video clip, bring some newspapers along instead. Ask people to find stories in which someone needs to be freed in some way and discuss them.

2   Pharaoh is unimpressed with the plague of blood because his magicians can do the same thing. He says he will let the people go after the plague of frogs but changes his mind when the frogs disappear. The magicians cannot produce gnats and recognise that God is at work. God makes a distinction between the Israelites and the Egyptians – the Israelites don't suffer the plagues. After the flies, Pharaoh says they can worship God in Egypt, then they can go if they don't go too far, but he goes back on his word again when the flies disappear. God gives the Egyptians the chance to escape the plague of hail, but only if they listen to what he says. Pharaoh offers a partial surrender again, but doesn't want them taking their flocks. He gets really angry with Moses. It takes the death of the firstborn Egyptians before he at last gives in and lets the Israelites go.

3   The Bible also says that Pharaoh and his officials hardened their own hearts (see Ex. 8:15, 32). Show people some ice and some clay and ask them to think about the different effect that a source of heat will have on each. Heat melts ice, but hardens clay. Does this help to explain the phrase, 'The Lord hardened Pharaoh's heart?'

4   This is a story of spiritual warfare, part of God's campaign against the forces of evil and his plan to redeem his whole creation from the effects of the fall.

5   Jesus has freed us from sin and death. He has freed us from the old covenant – the need to obey the law and make sacrifices.

6   Jesus' death on the cross has not just won our personal salvation. It has redeemed the whole creation from the effects of the fall. Not only can we have a restored relationship with God, but we look forward to a new heavens and a new earth, when the whole creation will be renewed and we will live in close relationship with God.

7   It's a question of what we do with our freedom. As Paul says in Galatians, we are not to abuse our freedom by indulging in sin, but we have the chance to offer that freedom back to God to live in the way that pleases him. We had no choice about whether we were slaves to sin or not; but we can choose to submit to God's ways and enjoy the benefits that brings.

8   Your answer will depend on your church! Some strands of the church emphasise the need for social and political freedom in a way that means their voice is not distinctive from many secular organisations. Other strands will emphasise the need for spiritual freedom and evangelism, and are in danger of ignoring the very real needs of people in poverty and oppression. We mustn't over-spiritualise the Exodus narrative, nor see it as a metaphor for any and every movement towards freedom.

WORSHIP

You need to decide whether your group know each other well enough to talk about the knots in their strings, or whether they should just pray generally for each other. Encourage people to continue to pray for each other outside of the housegroup.

SESSION 6 – Hope

MATERIALS NEEDED

A large bowl of sand, slips of paper and pens, glasses and jugs of water, or a copy of U2's album Rattle and Hum and something to play it on.

FEEDBACK

Did people find they were more aware of issues of poverty and injustice in the week?

TO SET THE SCENE

Many films give a high-tech view of the future – like Minority Report; a space-age view – like Star Trek; or a vision of disaster and a struggle for survival – like Waterworld. Many people have a bleak view of the future, fearing war, the spread of AIDS and further environmental destruction. Some people do believe that the advance of science will give us more control of our destiny and a better future, but this will probably only help those who are already rich and powerful – which, of course, includes most of us in the west. For the majority of the world's people, the expectation is that life will continue but will be worse.

1 God has brought them out of Egypt, although the decisive victory over the Egyptians is yet to be won. He has made them his own people, although they have yet to be given the law and have not had much time to worship him or get to know him. They have yet to arrive in the Promised Land.

2 Joseph, one of their ancestors, had hoped long ago that one day the Israelites would leave Egypt for their own land. Moses is taking Joseph's bones with him as Joseph requested. The Israelites have a pillar of fire by night and a pillar of cloud by day as visible signs of God's presence with them. You could also argue the fact that God didn't lead them through Philistine country shows that he knows their limits and this will give them hope that he will take care of them.

3 Our use of the word hope rarely carries much expectation that things will change. In contrast, biblical hope is confident and certain, talking about a future reality rather than a vague wish for something better.

4 Three times Paul says that we are given the Holy Spirit as a deposit guaranteeing our inheritance.

7 This type of desert experience is not a deliberate withdrawal to a solitary

place to spend time with God, but something that is not chosen. The Israelites grumbled a lot in the desert, a fact that can make them seem ungrateful and childish, but perhaps that shows just what a difficult place it was for them to be.

8   One key is to be real about our own experiences – not feeling that we have to 'talk-up' the gospel to make it seem more attractive or that if we admit to struggling at times then we have let God down. We also need to have a genuine sense of excitement about the future that God has prepared for us. Encourage people to look at the subject under the 'For further study' section.

WORSHIP

Provide a large bowl of sand, some slips of paper and pens. Ask people to think of someone who they know is going through a desert experience – which could be themselves – and write a prayer to God on the paper for that person. Invite them to bury the prayer in the sand, and take some sand to put in their pockets as a prompt to remind them to continue to pray. Provide glasses of cool water for people to drink.

Alternatively, you could play the track 'I still haven't found what I'm looking for' from U2's album Rattle and Hum. This is a wonderful expression of the 'now-but-not-yet' nature of our experience of the kingdom, and a holy restlessness to see more of God's reality. Invite people to pray afterwards, thanking God for what he has done in their lives and asking him to continue to work in them, in the church and in the world.

SESSION 7 – Worship

MATERIALS NEEDED

Art materials such as paints, pens, paper, pastels, clay, collage materials.

FEEDBACK

Who was able to pass on hope – or had hope passed on to them?

TO SET THE SCENE

Jamie Oliver may be known for his 'bung it all in' cooking; Davina McCall for her 'motherly' TV presenting, where she is always comforting disappointed would-be pop stars; Gary Lineker for his Match of the Day punditry and Walkers crisps adverts. People can describe actions or repeat catchphrases if they are not keen on acting. The link with this week's theme is that the Israelites too would be distinguished by their actions – in the centrality of worship to their corporate and personal lives.

1 They have learned that the Lord is the source of their salvation (v2), that he is powerful (v6,7), that the Egyptians were no match for him in spite of their boasts (v9,10), that he is unique (v11) and loving (v13) and that he will provide future security for them (v14-18).

2 Exodus 3:12 – when God first speaks to Moses, he says that Moses will worship him on this mountain once he has led the Israelites out of Egypt; Exodus 4:23 – Pharaoh is to be told that the reason for letting the Israelites go is so that they can worship God; Exodus 5:3 – Moses and Aaron request that the Israelites go to worship God at an event, their real intent being they should be set free for a life of worship; Exodus 15:1-18 – the song of worship that we have read; Exodus 20:1,2 – the first commandment is that the Israelites shall have no other God, the second is that they worship only Yahweh; Exodus 29:44-46 – God says he has brought the Israelites out of Egypt so that he might live among them – their lives will centre on worship.

3 The place where people worship will be less important than the manner in which they worship. God wants sincere, heartfelt worship, not religious habits.

4 We are to worship with our lives, not just our songs or our words; acts of mission and mercy can enhance worship. Secondly, worship needs to be at the heart of mission, so that our actions flow from our relationship with God. The third quote is very clear – worship is the goal of mission.

6   Yahweh is the one true God, unique and powerful. The tabernacle's central position in the camp echoes the centrality of worship to the Israelite's lives – worship is not an optional extra but core to who they are. God will be with his people as they travel. He is not restricted to one geographical area and reigns over the whole earth. The Israelites are to worship him wherever they go.

7   Bezalel was filled with the Spirit of God to be a craftsman, to use his gifts and creative ability to beautify the temple.

8   Many people are using rediscovering the use of arts in worship. Visit www.smallfire.org to see photos of some alternative worship services.

WORSHIP

Provide some art materials: paints, pens, paper, pastels or clay. Invite people to use these materials to create some artwork based on Exodus 15:1-18, that expresses worship to God. They could draw a picture, a cartoon, a pattern, or swirls of colour, or write a poem or psalm. If people have not done this before, they may protest that they are 'not creative' – but encourage them to have a go and pray as they are creating something. Allow half an hour, and then get everyone to bring their offerings to a central space. Even if people haven't actually 'produced' anything they will have spent some time in prayer and personal worship of God. People can talk about what they have done if they want to – but they shouldn't feel that they have to, nor that it has to have a specific meaning. Simply present these offerings to God and invite a few people to pray.

FURTHER INFORMATION

If you would like further information and resources, the following organisations may be of help. They will be able to tell you what is going on in your locality and how you can get involved:

The Evangelical Alliance
186 Kennington Park Road London SE11 4BT
tel – 020 7207 2100
email – info@eauk.org

Care for the Family
PO Box 488 Cardiff CF15 7YY
tel – 029 2081 0800
email – mail@cff.org.uk

Faithworks
tel – 0207 450 9050
www.faithworkscampaign.org

Open Doors
PO Box 6 Witney Oxon OX29 6WG
tel – 01993 885400
email – helpdesk@opendoorsuk.org

Rebuild
16 Kingston Road London SW19 1JZ
tel – 020 82395581
email – info@rebuild.org.uk

TEARFUND
100 Church Rd Teddington TW11 8QE
tel – 020 8977 9144
www.tearfund.org

NOTES

NOTES

NOTES